The ENGLISH COLLECTION

D1795103

GETTING INTO SHAKESPEARE

Theresa Sullivan

LONGMAN

CONTENTS

The English Collection

To the pupil

This series is for your pleasure and your profit. It's like a do-it-yourself kit – but with clear instructions.

Our main hope for the series is that you enjoy doing the reading, writing, talking and listening it involves. This has been an important consideration in choosing material. But, of course, we also need to help you fulfil the requirements of GCSE and the National Curriculum. The range of work will give you opportunities to develop your ability in every aspect of English, including assessment of your own progress – watch for the 'Look Back' headings in each section.

We want you to make – to create for yourself–
 stories
 poems
 advertisements
 magazine articles
 letters
 plays –
a full variety of styles of writing.

Each book in this series takes you carefully through the creation process, working individually, in small groups or as a complete class, helping you to –
 prepare
 discuss
 develop ideas
 plan
 redraft –
so that your final pieces are presented with clarity and care.

At the same time, you will be showing your ability to read –
 fiction
 non-fiction
 between the lines
 with discrimination
 aloud or silently.

You will be talking to different people in different situations –
 your classmates
 your teachers
 members of your community.

You will show that you understand that speech varies with context, and that you can listen sensitively and with comprehension to a variety of people.

READING, WRITING, SPEAKING and LISTENING – these are the three main aspects of the National Curriculum. The English Collection will help you make the most of your ability in each of them.

⟿ indicates a piece of writing

⟿ indicates oral work

Programmes of Study in Key Stage 4 that are covered in
Getting into Shakespeare

Speaking and listening

Pupils should be given opportunities to:

- express and justify feelings, opinions and viewpoints with increasing sophistication
- recount events and narrate stories
- respond to increasingly complex instructions and questions
- listen and respond to a range of plays
- recite and read aloud with increasing fluency and awareness of audience
- work with or devise an increasing range of drama scripts, taking on a variety of dramatic roles
- use, and understand the use of, role-play in teaching and learning
- communicate with other group members in a wide range of situations

Reading

Pupils should be given opportunities to:

- read some of the works of Shakespeare
- understand some of the main characteristics of literary language and how it conveys meaning
- understand some of the ways in which English is constantly changing between generations and over the centuries
- use the evidence in a text to interpret and form judgements about characters' motives and be able to quote evidence in support of their views
- discuss the themes, settings and characters of the texts they read in order to make a personal response to them

Writing

Pupils should be given opportunities to:

- write in a range of forms
- handle the elements of story structure – opening, setting, characters, events and resolution
- write in aesthetic and imaginative ways
- develop an increasingly varied and differentiated vocabulary
- record their first thoughts and collect and organise ideas

1

STARTING THE PLAY

—

Shakespeare wrote nearly forty plays in all. Most of the plots he used he did not invent himself; he found suitable stories and then reshaped them to suit himself. If you were to compare the original stories with Shakespeare's own versions, you would see how greatly Shakespeare had improved on them. He was an artist with a great deal of skill who knew how to keep the interest of the audience in the way that he structured his plays.

Finding the right place to start the play was obviously of crucial importance. Most of Shakespeare's opening scenes contain the seeds of what is to happen in the play – not just in terms of plot, but of the development of character and of theme as well.

The opening scene of *Macbeth*

➤ In pairs, read the opening scene of *Macbeth* and make a list of everything you learn from the scene. Then compare your list with the list over the page.

Macbeth: from Act 1, Scene 1

Thunder and lightning. Enter three witches.

FIRST WITCH
> When shall we three meet again?
> In thunder, lightning, or in rain?

SECOND WITCH
> When the hurly-burly's done,
> When the battle's lost and won.

THIRD WITCH
> That will be ere the set of sun.

FIRST WITCH
> Where the place?

SECOND WITCH
> Upon the heath.

THIRD WITCH
> There to meet with Macbeth.

FIRST WITCH
> I come, Grey-Malkin.

SECOND WITCH
> Paddock calls!

THIRD WITCH
> Anon!

ALL
> Fair is foul, and foul is fair.
> Hover through the fog and filthy air.

Exeunt

What we learn from this scene

1 The stage instructions say 'Thunder and lightning'. This suggests a terrifying, menacing atmosphere.
2 The second instruction is 'Enter three witches'. We associate witches with evil and a desire to do harm.
3 They talk about a battle. So is there a war going on? They talk about a battle being lost and won. How is that possible?
4 The witches agree to meet at sunset (night is traditionally the time for evil) and on the heath – a bare bleak place.
5 They are meeting Macbeth. Is he the person to whom they wish to do harm?
6 They talk of hovering through the fog and filthy air, suggesting a murky atmosphere where evil can be done unnoticed. Do they also have the power to fly?
7 They say 'Fair is foul, and foul is fair'. This is contradictory, like the battle being lost and won. What do they mean? That they can make good look like evil and evil like good?

LOOK BACK

How close was your list to the one above? If this is your first look at Shakespeare, your list may not be as detailed. As you become more used to Shakespeare's language, try to get into the habit of studying the extracts as closely as possible and making your answers as full as possible. You will find that it is the best way to understand and enjoy Shakespeare's plays.

Staging the scene

In threes, decide how you would ideally stage this scene (given unlimited money, lights, costume, make-up, special effects, etc). You can choose whether you produce it for a theatre or for a film. Make notes and diagrams of your decisions. Compare your production ideas with those of other groups.

Acting it out

In threes, learn the lines and act them out with the resources that you have. In Shakespeare's time, there would have been little in the way of staging, lighting, scenery or costume. The power of the performance would rest almost entirely on the actor's skill in moving and speaking the lines. See what you can do to produce the atmosphere. Show your scene to other groups and ask for their comments and suggestions. Did you find that learning the lines made it easier to understand and appreciate them?

What happens next?

If you want to know what happens when the witches meet Macbeth, then Shakespeare has succeeded in arousing your interest in the first scene of his play. It isn't the purpose of this book to study a complete play, but if you want to know more about a play that arouses your curiosity, then there are several ways in which you can satisfy that curiosity:

1 There are books specially written for both adults and children which give the stories of Shakespeare's plays. Ask your librarian.
2 There are videos of all of the plays. Again, ask your librarian or your teacher.
3 Read the play itself. You can get copies from your library or your teacher or a bookshop. You may find the language difficult, but it is worth persevering.
4 Many theatre companies perform Shakespeare's plays. You may be lucky to find a production in your area. The Royal Shakespeare Company at Stratford and at the Barbican in London performs over half a dozen Shakespeare plays a year.

The opening in *King Lear*

➤ In groups of four to six, read the following outline of what happens at the beginning of *King Lear*. Then improvise the scene, making sure that you include the lines given below. The characters you will need are Lear, Goneril, Regan, and Cordelia. If you have a larger group, then you can include the husbands of Goneril and Regan. As you work on your improvisation, decide upon what sort of characters the king and his three daughters are. What do you think of the situations the king has set up?

The outline

King Lear, an old man, has decided to divide his kingdom up and to pass his responsibilities on to his daughters' husbands while he passes his time peacefully until his death. A great ceremony is held in court: the king is on his throne holding a map. He asks:

> 'Tell me, my daughters,
> Which of you shall we say doth love us most?'

and tells them that whoever gives the best answer will gain the biggest share of the land on the map.
Goneril, the first-born, is the first to speak. She tells her father:

> 'Sir, I love you more than word can wield the matter;
> Dearer than eye-sight, space and liberty;'

Lear is pleased with her answer and points out on the map how much land she has won.
Next Regan speaks:

> 'In my true heart
> I find she names my very deed of love;
> Only she comes too short.'

She, too, is given an ample third of the kingdom. Now Lear calls upon his 'joy', his youngest daughter, to declare her love. He expects her to win the most 'opulent' (richest) third of the kingdom. Cordelia says: 'Nothing, my lord.' Lear asks her to speak again: if she does not 'mend' (improve) her speech, she will 'mar' (spoil) her fortunes. Cordelia says:

> 'Unhappy that I am, I cannot heave
> My heart into my mouth: I love your Majesty
> According to my bond; no more nor less.'

LOOK BACK

What did you decide about the characters and the situation?
Watch the work of other groups. What similarities were there?
What differences?

➤ Compare your improvisation with Shakespeare's actual scene. What differences are there? What similarities? To help you in your understanding of the scene, the definitions of the underlined words are given below the extract.

King Lear: from Act 1, Scene 1

LEAR

                                  Tell me, my daughters,
Which of you shall we say doth love us most?
That we our largest bounty may extend
Where nature doth with merit challenge. Goneril,
Our eldest-born, speak first.

GONERIL

Sir, I love you more than word can <u>wield the matter</u>;
Dearer than eye-sight, space and liberty;
Beyond what can be valued rich or rare;
No less than life, with grace, health, beauty, honour;
As much as child e'er lov'd, or father found;
A love that makes breath poor and speech unable;
Beyond all manner of so much I love you.

CORDELIA

(*Aside*.) What shall Cordelia speak? Love, and be
    silent.

LEAR

Of all these <u>bounds</u>, even from this line to this,
With shadowy forests and with <u>champains</u> rich'd,
With plenteous rivers and wide-skirted <u>meads</u>,
We make thee lady: to thine and Albany's <u>issues</u>
Be this perpetual. What says our second daughter
Our dearest Regan, wife of Cornwall?

REGAN

I am made of that self metal as my sister,
And prize me at her worth. In my true heart
I find she names my very deed of love;
Only she comes too short: that I profess
Myself an enemy to all other joys
Which the most precious square of sense possesses,
And find I am alone <u>felicitate</u>
In your dear highness' love.

CORDELIA

                      (*Aside*.) Then poor Cordelia!
And yet not so; since I am sure my love's
More ponderous than my tongue.

LEAR

To thee and thine, hereditary ever,
Remain this ample third of our fair kingdom,
No less in space, validity, and pleasure,
Than that conferr'd on Goneril. Now, our joy,
Although our last, and least; to whose young love
The vines of France and milk of Burgundy
Strive <u>to be interess'd</u>; what can you say to draw
A third more opulent than your sisters? Speak.

CORDELIA

Nothing, my lord.

LEAR

Nothing?

CORDELIA

Nothing.

LEAR

Nothing will come of nothing; speak again.

CORDELIA

Unhappy that I am, I cannot heave
My heart into my mouth: I love your Majesty
According to my bond; no more nor less.

LEAR

How, how, Cordelia! Mend your speech a little,
Lest you may mar your fortunes.

CORDELIA

                           Good, my Lord,
You have begot me, bred me, lov'd me: I
Return those duties back as are right fit,
Obey you, love you, and most honour you.
Why have my sisters husbands, if they say
They love you all? Haply, when I shall wed,
That lord whose hand must take my <u>plight</u> shall carry
Half my love with him, half my care and duty;
Sure I shall never marry like my sisters,
To love my father all.

LEAR

But goes thy heart with this?

CORDELIA

                      Ay, my good Lord.

LEAR

So young, and so untender?

CORDELIA

So young, my Lord, and true.

<u>wield the matter</u> – express
<u>bounds</u> – boundaries
<u>champains</u> – meadows
<u>meads</u> – meadows
<u>issues</u> – children
<u>felicitate</u> – fortunate
<u>to be interess'd</u> – to possess
<u>plight</u> – wedding vow

In your groups, discuss the following:

Comment on Goneril's speech. What would you criticise about it as a declaration of love? Comment in the same way on Regan's speech. How might you tell that the speeches have been prepared before-hand?

How can you tell that Cordelia is anxious about having to speak herself? What is your opinion of her answer? Do you think she does love her father best, as he originally thought? What would you say if your father put you in this position?

What happens next?

Cordelia is banished for her plain-speaking. The King of France still wishes to marry her even though she has no money or land. Lear declares that he will stay with each of his other two daughters in turn. That is the position at the end of the first scene. In pairs, decide what you think will happen next.

Comedy – the opening scene of *Twelfth Night*

The opening scenes of *Macbeth* and *King Lear* prepare us to expect that tragedy will follow, either by creating a sense of evil or by showing a foolish action which must have tragic consequences. The opening of *Twelfth Night*, however, prepares us for things to happen by coincidence, for characters to be in love, to suffer strange adventures, and to be in disguise – all things we expect to happen in comedy. First read the opening scene.

Twelfth Night: from Act 1, Scene 1

A room in the Duke's palace.
Music. Enter Orsino Duke of Illyria, Curio, and other lords.

ORSINO
  If music be the food of love, play on,
  Give me excess of it, that, surfeiting,
  The appetite may sicken, and so die.
  That strain again! It had a dying fall.
  O, it came o'er my ear like the sweet sound
  That breathes upon a bank of violets,
  Stealing and giving odour. Enough, no more!
  'Tis not so sweet now as it was before.

  O, when mine eyes did see Olivia first,
  Methought she purged the air of pestilence.

Enter Valentine.

  (*To Valentine*)
  How now! What news from her?
VALENTINE
  So please my lord, I might not be admitted,
  But from her handmaid do return this answer:
  The element itself, till seven years' heat,
  Shall not behold her face at ample view,
  But like a cloistress she will veilèd walk,
  And water once a day her chamber round
  With eye-offending brine; all this to season
  A brother's dead love, which she would keep fresh
  And lasting, in her sad remembrance.
ORSINO
  O, she that hath a heart of that fine frame
  To pay this debt of love but to a brother –
  How will she love, when the rich golden shaft
  Hath killed the flock of all affections else
  That live in her; when liver, brain, and heart,
  These sovereign thrones, are all supplied and filled –
  Her sweet perfections – with one self king!
  Away before me to sweet beds of flowers!
  Love thoughts lie rich when canopied with bowers.

  Exeunt

surfeiting – eating too much
strain – tune
element – sky
cloistress – nun
brine – tears
season – honour

Orsino is in love. Do you think he is genuinely in love, or do you thinking he is posing? What power does music have for him? Olivia, the woman Orsino is love-sick for, has sent him a message saying that she will not leave her house or stop her mourning for seven years. Who is she mourning for? Orsino draws comfort from the fact that she loves her brother so much. What comfort does he draw?

Twelfth Night: from Act 1, Scene 2

The sea-coast.
Enter Viola, a Captain, and sailors.

VIOLA
  What country, friends, is this?

CAPTAIN
  This is Illyria, lady.

VIOLA
  And what should I do in Illyria?
  My brother, he is in Elysium.
  Perchance he is not drowned. What think you, sailors?

CAPTAIN
  It is perchance that you yourself were saved.

VIOLA
  O, my poor brother! and so perchance may he be.

CAPTAIN
  True, madam, and to comfort you with chance,
  Assure yourself, after our ship did split,
  When you and those poor number saved with you
  Hung on our driving boat, I saw your brother,
  Most provident in peril, bind himself –
  Courage and hope both teaching him the practice –
  To a strong mast, that lived upon the sea;
  Where, like Arion on the dolphin's back,
  I saw him hold acquaintance with the waves
  So long as I could see.

VIOLA
  For saying so, there's gold.
  Mine own escape unfoldeth to my hope,
  Whereto thy speech serves for authority,
  The like of him. Knowest thou this country?

CAPTAIN
  Ay, madam, well, for I was bred and born
  Not three hours' travel from this very place.

VIOLA
  Who governs here?

CAPTAIN
  A noble Duke, in nature as in name.

VIOLA
  What is his name?

CAPTAIN
  Orsino.

VIOLA
  Orsino…I have heard my father name him.
  He was a bachelor then.

CAPTAIN
  And so is now, or was so, very late;

For but a month ago I went from hence,
And then 'twas fresh in murmur – as you know,
What great ones do, the less will prattle of –
That he did seek the love of fair Olivia.

VIOLA
  What's she?

CAPTAIN
  A virtuous maid, the daughter of a count
  That died some twelvemonth since, then leaving her
  In the protection of his son, her brother,
  Who shortly also died; for whose dear love,
  They say, she hath abjured the sight
  And company of men.

VIOLA
  O, that I served that lady,
  And might not be delivered to the world –
  Till I had made mine own occasion mellow –
  What my estate is.

CAPTAIN
  That were hard to compass,
  Because she will admit no kind of suit,
  No, not the Duke's.

VIOLA
  I prithee – and I'll pay thee bounteously –
  Conceal me what I am, and be my aid
  For such diguise as haply shall become
  The form of my intent. I'll serve this Duke.
  Thou shalt present me as an eunuch to him.
  It may be worth thy pains, for I can sing
  And speak to him in many sorts of music
  That will allow me very worth his service.
  What else may hap to time I will commit.
  Only shape thou thy silence to my wit.

abjured – given up
delivered – made known
made mine own occasion mellow – created an
opportunity to show
estate – true rank
compass – arrange
suit – request
haply – perhaps
intent – intention

By coincidence, a young woman, Viola, has just been shipwrecked off the coast of Illyria, where Duke Orsino rules. She has lost her brother (who is in fact her twin) in the wreck – or so she thinks. What hope does the captain give her that he is still alive? Do you think that it is likely that he is alive or dead?

She learns from the captain what we found out in the previous scene, and decides to disguise herself as a boy in order to serve Orsino as his eunuch or page.

You now know three names – Viola, Olivia and Orsino (who is in love with Olivia). The play is about love and concerns a love triangle between these three characters. Who, therefore, do you think falls in love with whom? There is a clue in the second scene about how this unfortunate situation may be resolved. Can you work out what it is and therefore what the ending of the play might be?

Staging the scene

Until about fifty years ago, it was usual to stage Shakespeare's plays very lavishly with lots of sets and changes of scenery. This meant long and frequent waits for the audience which slowed the action of the play, because Shakespeare changes his location so often. But in his time, staging was very simple – an open stage, a few props to suggest location and no lighting since the theatre was open to the air. Nowadays theatre groups have returned to this simple staging, but with the additional resources of lighting and sound effects.

✍ In pairs, think about how you would stage the two opening scenes of *Twelfth Night* to bring out the contrast between the two locations and the different atmospheres of the two scenes. Think in terms of an empty stage, a few props, and whatever lighting and sound effects you might need. Make notes and diagrams of your staging.

Now that you have looked at a few of Shakespeare's opening scenes, you will have realised that he uses them to convey basic information – about names and situations – that the audience needs to know.

Your own opening scene – *Julius Caesar*

✍ Here is the basic information given in the first scene of *Julius Caesar*. Read it through and write your opening scene to *Julius Caesar*, making sure that you include all the necessary information.

1 A crowd of Roman citizens are out celebrating in the streets.
2 Flavius and Marullus, who are tribunes (officers), tell them to go home because it is not a holiday.
3 They ask two men what their occupation is. One says he is a carpenter; the other a cobbler.
4 The tribunes tell them to get back to their work.
5 The cobbler tells them that they are out celebrating Caesar's victory over another leader called Pompey.
6 Marullus is angry at the changeable nature of the crowd. It wasn't long ago that they were out celebrating Pompey's victories and climbing up to the chimney pots to catch a sight of him returning to Rome. Now they are celebrating because Pompey is dead.
7 Flavius tells the crowd to go to the banks of the River Tiber and there weep for Pompey.
8 The crowd quietly leaves.
9 Flavius tells Marullus to remove all signs and trophies in support of Caesar, while he continues to drive people from the streets. Otherwise it will encourage Caesar in his growing greatness. He is afraid that Caesar will want to become king.

LOOK BACK

Now compare your version of the scene with Shakespeare's (page 15). What similarities are there? What differences? In what ways do you think Shakespeare's version is better than yours? The play is about Julius Caesar's assassination: how does the opening scene prepare us for what is to happen later? What are the different attitudes to Caesar that you learn about in the scene? Why do you think many people in Rome want to kill Caesar?

Julius Caesar: from Act 1, Scene 1

Enter Flavius, Marullus, and certain commoners over the stage.

FLAVIUS
Hence! home, you idle creatures, get you home:
Is this a holiday? What, know you not,
Being <u>mechanical</u>, you ought not walk
Upon a labouring day without the sign
Of your profession? Speak, what trade art thou?

CARPENTER
Why, sir, a carpenter.

MARULLUS
Where is thy leather apron, and thy rule?
What dost thou with thy best apparel on?
You, sir, what trade are you?

COBBLER
Truly, sir, in respect of a fine workman, I am but, as
you would say, a cobbler.

FLAVIUS
But wherefore art not in thy shop today?
Why dost thou lead these men about the streets?

COBBLER
Truly, sir, to wear out their shoes to get myself into
more work. But indeed, sir, we make holiday to see
Caesar, and to rejoice in his triumph.

MARULLUS
Wherefore rejoice? What conquest brings he home?
What <u>tributaries</u> follow him to Rome,
To grace in captive bonds his chariot wheels?
You blocks, you stones, you worse than senseless
  things!
O you hard hearts, you cruel men of Rome,
Knew you not Pompey? Many a time and oft
Have you climbed up to walls and battlements,
To towers and windows, yea, to chimney-tops,
Your infants in your arms, and there have sat
The livelong day, with patient expectation,
To see great Pompey pass the streets of Rome:
And when you saw his chariot but appear,
Have you not made an universal shout,
That Tiber trembled underneath her banks
To hear the replication of your sounds
Made in her concave shores?

And do you now put on your best attire?
And do you now cull out a holiday?
And do you now strew flowers in his way,
That comes in triumph over Pompey's blood?
Be gone!
Run to your houses, fall upon your knees,
Pray to the gods to <u>intermit</u> the plague
That needs must light on this ingratitude.

FLAVIUS
Go, go, good countrymen, and for this fault
Assemble all the poor men of your sort;
Draw them to Tiber banks, and weep your tears
Into the channel, till the lowest stream
Do kiss the most exalted shores of all.
                              Exeunt all the commoners
See where their <u>basest mettle</u> be not moved.
They vanish tongue-tied in their guiltiness.
Go you down that way towards the Capitol;
This way will I. Disrobe the images,
If you do find them decked with ceremonies.

MARULLUS
May we do so?
You know it is the feast of Lupercal.

FLAVIUS
It is no matter; let no images
Be hung with Caesar's trophies. I'll about,
And drive away the <u>vulgar</u> from the streets;
So do you too, where you perceive them <u>thick</u>.
These growing feathers plucked from Caesar's wing
Will make him fly an ordinary pitch,
Who else would soar above the view of men,
And keep us all in servile fearfulness.
                                        Exeunt

<u>mechanical</u> – a workman
<u>tributaries</u> – payers of tribute
<u>intermit</u> – keep off
<u>basest mettle</u> – low natures
<u>vulgar</u> – common people
<u>thick</u> – in large numbers

Choose another of Shakespeare's plays and
look at the way he unfolds the story in the first
few scenes. Again, make a list of everything you
learn at the beginning of the play.

LOOK BACK

What have you learned about the different
ways Shakespeare uses to start a play?

2

HOW SHAKESPEARE CREATES CHARACTER

How does Shakespeare tell us about the characters he has created? He has several ways in which he can do this. The simplest is to have the character talk to us directly – this is called 'soliloquy'. He can also reveal to us what a character is like by showing him or her talking to one or more other characters. Or he can show the character in action – what the character does tells us about what he or she is like.

But the most important thing of all to remember about Shakespeare's characters is that they all have a distinctive way of speaking that makes them immediately recognisable. Each character sounds different from any other character. So it is particularly important in this chapter to read out the extracts so that you can hear the characters speaking.

A soliloquy

One of the ways Shakespeare tells us about characters is the soliloquy – the character tells us directly about him or herself. Richard of Gloucester reveals in the following speech to the audience his great ambition to become king. At present, however, his brother has just been crowned Edward VI and, since he has several sons, it seems unlikely that Richard will ever become king. But, by plotting and scheming and murdering everyone in his way, Richard does eventually become King Richard III. Here, for the first time on stage, he reveals his potential as a villain.

Henry VI, Part III: from Act 3, Scene 2

RICHARD

Ay, Edward will use women honourably,
Would he were wasted, marrow, bones, and all,
That from his loins <u>no hopeful branch</u> may spring,
To cross me from the golden time I look for!
And yet, between my soul's desire and me –
The lustful Edward's title buried, –
130 Is Clarence, Henry and his son young Edward,
Add all the <u>unlook'd for issue</u> of their bodies,
To take their rooms, ere I can place myself:
A cold premeditation for my purpose!
Why then, I do but dream of sovereignty;
Like one that stands upon a promontory,
And spies a far-off shore where he would tread,
Wishing his foot were equal with his eye;
And chides the sea that sunders him from thence,
Saying, he'll lade it dry to have his way:
140 So do I wish the crown, being so far off,
And so I chide the means that keep me from it,
And so I say I'll cut the causes off,
Flattering me with impossibilities,
My eye's too quick, my heart o'erweens too much,
Unless my hand and strength could equal them.
Well, say there is no kingdom then for Richard;
What other pleasure can the world afford?
I'll make my heaven in a lady's lap,
And deck my body in gay ornaments,
150 And witch sweet ladies with my words and looks.
O miserable thought! and more unlikely
Than to accomplish twenty golden crowns,
Why, love <u>forswore</u> me in my mother's womb;
And, for I should not deal in her soft laws,
She did corrupt frail nature with some bribe,
To shrink mine arm up like a wither'd shrub;
To make an envious mountain on my back,
Where sits deformity to mock my body;
To shape my legs of an unequal size;
160 To disproportion me in every part,
Like to a chaos, or an unlick'd bear-<u>whelp</u>
That carries no impression like the <u>dam</u>.

And am I then a man to be belov'd?
O monstrous fault! to harbour such a thought.
Then, since this earth affords no joy to me
But to command, to check, to o'erbear such
As are of better person than myself,
I'll make my heaven to dream upon the crown,
And, whiles I live, t'account this world but hell,
170 Until my misshaped trunk that bears this head
Be round impaled with a glorious crown.
And yet I know not how to get the crown,
For many lives stand between me and home;
And I – like one lost in a thorny wood,
That rents the thorns and is rent with the thorns,
Seeking a way and straying from the way,
Not knowing how to find the open air,
But toiling desperately to find it out –
Torment myself to catch the English crown;
180 And from that torment I will free myself,
Or hew my way out with a bloody axe.
Why, I can smile, and murder whiles I smile,
And cry 'Content!' to that which grieves my heart,
And wet my cheeks with artificial tears,
And frame my face to all occasions.
I'll drown more sailors than the mermaid shall;
I'll slay more gazers than the basilisk;
I'll play the orator as well as Nestor,
Deceive more slily than Ulysses could,
190 And, like a Sinon, take another Troy.
I can add colours to the chameleon,
Change shapes with Proteus for advantages,
And set the murderous Machiavel to school.
Can I do this, and cannot get a crown?
Tut, were it farther off, I'll pluck it down.

<u>no hopeful branch</u> – no heir
<u>unlook'd for issue</u> – unborn children
<u>forswore</u> – deserted
<u>whelp</u> – cub
<u>dam</u> – mother

Richard makes several points in the development of his argument that he will not rest until he wins the crown.

1 Richard lists Edward's sons and all his possible grandsons who stand between him and the throne. (lines 124–133)

2 He makes a comparison to show how far away he feels he is from being king. What is the comparison? (lines 134–143)

3 If he is not to be king, he will find another way of taking his pleasure. What is this other way? (lines 144–150)

4 Why does he then think that this way of enjoying himself is even more impossible and unlikely than becoming a king? What do you learn about his appearance? (lines 150–162)

5 What conclusion does he then make? (lines 163–168)

6 Having come to that conclusion, what is then the problem? What image does he use to show how he torments himself to get the crown? (lines 169–181)

7 What does he tell us about himself in this section? How does he show that he is a very determined character and a skilful deceiver? (lines 182–195)

Write a letter

↯ Imagine that you are a servant who has found and read Richard's diary in which he records his ambitions to be king. Write an anonymous letter to King Edward in which you outline your fears about Richard. Refer to him by his title, Duke of Gloucester. Use as much information as you can from the soliloquy. Include some comments about his appearance, and your fear that this might be the cause of Richard's ambition – that he cannot win the love of women.

'And yet I know not how to get the crown'

↯ In groups of four, find a way of acting out the lines from 'And yet . . .' to '. . . bloody axe' (lines 172–181). You may wish to repeat or to echo certain important lines or phrases to emphasise them.

A comic character

This long speech from Juliet's Nurse in *Romeo and Juliet* is not a soliloquy because she is talking to Juliet and her mother, Lady Capulet. But it is similar to a soliloquy because she does not allow either of them to interrupt her or to stop her in the middle of her reminiscences about Juliet's childhood. She remembers how she weaned Juliet using a bitter substance, wormwood, at the age of three, and how, the day before, Juliet fell over and hurt her forehead, which prompted a crude joke from the Nurse's husband.

Romeo and Juliet: from Act 1, Scene 3

NURSE
Even or odd, of all days in the year,
Come Lammas Eve at night shall she be fourteen.
Susan and she – God rest all Christian souls! –
Were of an age. Well, Susan is with God.
She was too good for me. But, as I said,
On Lammas Eve at night shall she be fourteen.
That shall she, marry! I remember it well.
'Tis since the earthquake now eleven years;
And she was weaned – I never shall forget it –
Of all the days of the year, upon that day.
For I had then laid wormwood to my dug,
Sitting in the sun under the dovehouse wall.
My lord and you were then at Mantua.
Nay, I do bear a brain. But, as I said,
When it did taste the wormwood on the nipple
Of my dug and felt it bitter, pretty fool,
To see it tetchy and fall out wi' th' dug!
And since that time it is eleven years.
For then she could stand high-lone. Nay, by th'rood,
She could have run and waddled all about.
For even the day before she broke her brow.
And then my husband – God be with his soul!
'A was a merry man – took up the child.
'Yea,' quoth he, 'dost thou fall upon thy face?
Thou wilt fall backward when thou hast more wit.
With thou not, Jule?' And, by my holidam,
The pretty wretch left crying and said 'Ay'.
To see now how a jest shall come about!
I warrant, an I should live a thousand years,
I never should forget it 'Wilt thou not, Jule?' quoth
    he,
And, pretty fool, it stinted and said 'Ay'.
LADY CAPULET
Enough of this. I pray thee hold thy peace.
NURSE
Yes, madam. Yet I cannot choose but laugh
To think it should leave crying and say 'Ay'.

wormwood – bitter herb
dug – breast
tetchy – angry
high-lone – by herself
th'rood – cross
an – if
stinted – stopped

How old is Juliet now? Who do you think Susan is? What is the husband's joke?

The Nurse's character

In her retelling of incidents from Juliet's childhood, Shakespeare allows the Nurse to tell us a great deal about herself. Find evidence to illustrate each of these characteristics of the Nurse:

rambling, repetitive, sentimental, pious, nostalgic, coarse, proud of and affectionate towards Juliet, good-natured, proud of her ability to remember.

Can you find other characteristics yourselves? What sort of accent do you imagine the Nurse to have? What do you imagine her to look like? What effect do you think she has on Lady Capulet?

Your own writing

Write a piece in which you say what impression Shakespeare meant us to have of the Nurse. Use quotations from the extract to illustrate the points you make.

Or imagine that the Nurse is no longer needed in the Capulet household and is applying for another job. Make up the reference that Lady Capulet might write about her to her possible new employers.

A character persuades

In *A Winter's Tale*, King Leontes is in a state of mad jealousy about his wife, Hermione. He has thrown her into prison, believing, completely wrongly, that she has been having an affair with his best friend, Polixenes. There she gives birth to a baby girl while awaiting her trial. Paulina, her faithful lady in waiting, has taken the baby from the prison to show it to the father in order to persuade him that it is his child and not his friend's.

Paulina is a forceful character who has pushed her way past the king's men in order to see him. She is filled with powerful indignation that Leontes should make such a dreadful mistake.

〰️ In your groups, discuss the following:

How does Paulina emphatically insist that Queen Hermione has done no wrong? What does she threaten to do to anyone who lays a hand on her? What is Leontes' reaction when she lays down the child in front of him? What does he order should happen to the child? How does Paulina try to persuade him that it is his child? Are you convinced by what she says? What does Leontes threaten to do to Paulina? How does she behave on her dignity when she is taken from the chamber?

A Winter's Tale: from Act 2, Scene 3

PAULINA
Good my liege, I come –
From your good queen.

LEONTES
Good queen?

PAULINA
Good queen, my lord, good queen, I say good queen;
And would by combat make her good, so were I
A man, the worst about you.

LEONTES
                                                    Force her hence.

PAULINA
Let him that makes but trifles of his eyes
First hand me. On mine own accord I'll off,
But first I'll do my errand. The good Queen –
For she is good – hath brought you forth a daughter:
Here 'tis; commends it to your blessing.
She lays down the child.

LEONTES
Out!
A mankind witch! Hence with her, out o'door!
A most intelligencing bawd!

LEONTES
                                                    A callat
Of boundless tongue, who late hath beat her husband,
And now baits me! This brat is none of mine:
It is the issue of Polixenes.
Hence with it, and together with the dam
Commit them to the fire!

PAULINA
It is yours;
And, might we lay th'old proverb to your charge,
So like you, 'tis the worse. Behold, my lords,
Although the print be little, the whole matter
And copy of the father: eye, nose, lip;
The trick of's frown; his forehead; nay, the valley,
The pretty dimples of his chin and cheek; his smiles;
The very mould and frame of hand, nail, finger.
And thou, good goddess Nature, which hast made it
So like to him that got it, if thou hast
The ordering of the mind too, 'mongst all colours
No yellow in't, lest she suspect, as he does,
Her children not her husband's.

LEONTES
I'll ha'thee burned.

PAULINA
I care not:
It is an heretic that makes the fire,

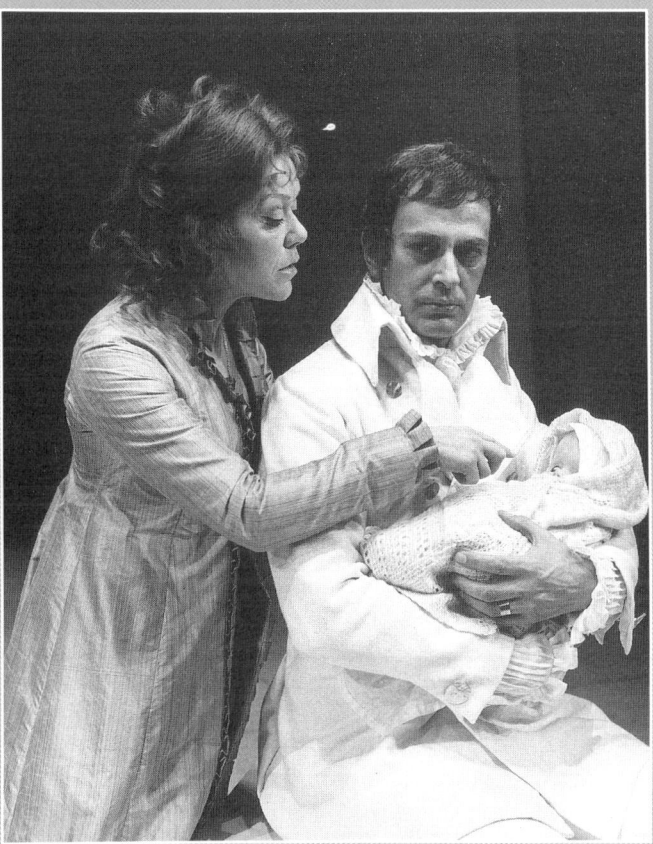

Not she which burns in't. I'll not call you tyrant;
But this most cruel usage of your queen –
Not able to produce more accusation
That your own weak-hinged fancy – something
    savours
Of tyranny, and will ignoble make you,
Yea, scandalous to the world.

LEONTES
On your allegiance,
Out of the chamber with her! Were I a tyrant,
Where were her life? She durst not call me so,
If she did know me one. Away with her!
They slowly push her towards the door.

PAULINA
I pray you, do not push me, I'll be gone.
Look to your babe, my lord; 'tis yours. Jove send her
A better guiding spirit! What needs these hands?
You that are thus so tender o'er his follies
Will never do him good, not one of you.
So, so. Farewell, we are gone.

                                    Exit

callat – nag

Paulina's function in the play

Paulina is a minor character. She is there for a purpose. She has a job to do in the play. What point do you think Shakespeare is making about the king's behaviour by having this scene with Paulina and the baby? Does it make the king seem more out of control and full of mad jealousy? Does her indignation reflect our indignation? Do you think her visit might have made the situation worse for Hermione and her baby?

Improvise the scene

In threes, look at this basic outline of the scene.

1 Paulina forces her way into the king's presence carrying the baby. (Use something to suggest the baby – a jumper formed into the right shape, for instance.)
2 She insists that the queen is innocent and good.
3 Leontes tries to have her removed.
4 Paulina threatens to tear out anybody's eyes who attempts it.
5 She presents the child to the king.
6 Leontes says it is not his child, but Polixenes' and threatens to burn it.
7 Paulina points out every feature of the baby's face which is identical to Leontes'.
8 Leontes threatens to burn her and orders his men to remove her.
9 Paulina refuses to be pushed and leaves, calling upon Leontes to look to his baby.

One person acts as narrator and tells the story of Paulina's visit to the king. The other two are Leontes and Paulina. Prepare nine still pictures showing each of the stages in the scene. When you have practised, show your work to the rest of your class.

LOOK BACK

What do you now feel about Leontes and Paulina, having improvised their scene together?
What do you think will happen next in the play?
Did improvising the scene help you to understand the extract more?

Paulina's language

Shakespeare chooses his words carefully to reveal and suit his characters. This makes them very recognisable. You have seen how Juliet's Nurse rambles when she is telling a story and how Shakespeare shows Richard justifying his murderous plans with false arguments. Paulina too has a very distinctive character.

✍ In groups of three, choose three things that Paulina says that particularly show her character. Each of you learn one of them. Try saying them in different ways and decide which way you like best. Now make a performance from just those three phrases or sentences. For instance, you could keep repeating them growing louder every time until you reach a climax. You could accompany each sentence with an appropriate gesture.

Your own writing

✍ Write the account that Paulina might give to Hermione when she returns to the prison with the baby. Make your account as detailed as possible. Use some of the language from the extract.

A character's past history

Sometimes Shakespeare wants to tell us about what has happened to a character before the play began. Occasionally, too, he creates fantastical characters who could not possibly exist in real life. In *The Tempest*, Prospero, once Duke of Milan, and his daughter, Miranda, are put to sea in a rotten old tub by his wicked brother. They are finally cast up on a remote island deserted except for two creatures, one of whom is Caliban, a monster born of a witch called Sycorax, and fathered by the devil. Caliban claims the island as his own because it used to belong to his mother. Prospero originally treated him with kindness, but since Caliban abused his kindness, he now treats him as his slave.

✍ In your groups, discuss the following:

1 What do we learn about the way Prospero treated Caliban from Caliban's opening speech?
2 Why, according to Prospero, did he stop treating Caliban in this way?
3 Prospero tried to educate Caliban. Can you infer, from the extract, what Caliban must have been like before?
4 What does Prospero threaten Caliban with if he refuses to obey him?

The Tempest: from Act 1, Scene 2

CALIBAN

This island's mine, by Sycorax my mother,
Which thou tak'st from me. When thou camest first,
Thou strok'dst me, and made much of me; wouldst
   give me
Water with berries in't; and teach me how
To name the bigger light, and how the less,
That burn by day and night: and then I lov'd thee
And show'd thee all the qualities o'th' isle,
The fresh springs, brine-pits, barren place, and fertile.
Cursed be I that did so! – All the charms
Of Sycorax, toads, beetles, bats, light on you!
For I am all the subjects that you have,
Which first was mine own king; and here you sty me
In this hard rock, whiles you do keep from me
The rest o' th' island.

PROSPERO

Thou most lying slave,
Whom stripes may move, not kindness! I have us'd
   thee,
Filth as thou art, with human care; and lodg'd thee
In mine own cell, till thou didst seek to violate
The honour of my child.

CALIBAN

Oh ho! Oh ho! – would it had been done!
Thou didst prevent me; I had peopled else
This isle with Calibans.

PROSPERO

Abhorred slave,
Which any print of goodness will not take,

Being capable of all ill! I pitied thee,
Took pains to make thee speak, taught thee each hour
One thing or other: when thou didst not, savage,
Know thine own meaning, but wouldst gabble like
A thing most brutish, I endow'd thy purposes
With words that made them known: but thy vile race,
Though thou didst learn, had that in't which good
   natures
Could not abide to be with; therefore wast thou
Deservedly confin'd into this rock,
Who hadst deserv'd more than a prison.

CALIBAN

You taught me language; and my profit on't
Is, I know how to curse: the red plague rid you,
For learning me your language!

PROSPERO

Hag-seed, hence!
Fetch us in fuel; and be quick, thou'rt best,
To answer other business. Shrug'st thou, malice?
If thou neglect'st, or dost unwillingly
What I command, I'll rack thee with old cramps,
Fill all thy bones with aches; make thee roar,
That beasts shall tremble at thy din.

CALIBAN

No, pray thee! –
[*Aside.*] I must obey: his art is of such power.

sty – imprison
stripes – whipping

Caliban's language

Caliban is clearly a monstrous creature, yet Shakespeare makes us feel some sympathy for him. Caliban spends much of his energy using his new found language to curse Prospero. But Shakespeare also gives him very simple child-like language which makes us feel sorry for him. Find some examples of this. Monster though he is, Caliban has some sense of the beauty of the island. Find examples of this.

In groups of four, divide the section from 'When thou camest first . . .' to '. . . and fertile' between you. Say the lines bringing out the gentle childlike side of Caliban in the way you say the words.

Then divide the section from 'Cursed be I . . .' to '. . . The rest o'th' island' between you. Again practise the lines, this time bringing out the ugly side of Caliban in the harsh way that you say the words.

Do you notice any difference in the quality of the sounds of the words in each section?

Learn your lines and perform them as a group, bringing out as much as you can the two sides of Caliban.

Your own drawings

1 Draw a picture of what you imagine Caliban to look like.
2 Caliban is an uneducated savage. He is a brute who would have raped Miranda. But at the same time Shakespeare gives him an innocence and a child-like quality. Draw the island as Caliban sees it and as he might draw it himself. Use as much of the information given in the extract as you can.

The actor playing Caliban

In pairs, discuss what sort of actor you would choose to play Caliban. How would you suggest he should move, speak, dress, make up in order to play the part? How successful do you think the portrayal of Caliban is in the photograph on page 23?

LOOK BACK

The point of this chapter has been to show that we learn about characters in Shakespeare's plays from the words they use. In groups of four, choose one phrase, sentence or line for each of the four characters you have looked at. Choose one of the four characters and decide upon a gesture or position which you think sums up that character. Present your character while another member of your group says your line or sentence. Present each character to the rest of the class in this way, and ask for their comments. Have you given a clear impression of that character?

3

ACTION ON STAGE

—

Audience love action on stage – and fight scenes provide plenty of excitement. In this section you will be studying two contrasting fight scenes from Shakespeare's plays.

A brawl from *Romeo and Juliet*

Understanding the story

✍ Act out the following:

1 Divide yourselves into two large groups. Half of you belong to the Capulet family, the other half to the Montagues. Each family stands at opposite ends of the room in a straight line facing the other family. The two families are enemies and will quarrel and fight at the slightest opportunity.

2 Learn or have with you the following lines of dialogue. Biting the thumb is an insulting gesture. You put your thumb nail in your mouth and jerk it from your top teeth, making a clicking sound. (What equivalent gestures are used today as a challenge to a fight at a football match or between gangs?)

CAPULETS
 Do you bite your thumb at us, sir?
MONTAGUES
 I do bite my thumb, sir.
CAPULETS
 Do you bite your thumb at us, sir?
MONTAGUES
 No, sir, I do not bite my thumb at you, sir. But I do bite my thumb, sir.

3 Now start speaking the lines. As each family speaks a line, the team takes one step forward. Keep repeating the lines until both families reach the centre of the room. Repeat, trying to make your voices and movements as threatening as you can. Now you are ready to look at the scene from which this little bit was taken.

The scene

The play opens with Sampson and Gregory, who are servants of the house of Capulet, challenging the servants of the enemy house of Montague to a fight. Gregory and Sampson see Abraham (a servant of the house of Montague) and his friend and decide to challenge them. First they discuss what they are going to do. The fight escalates. First their masters, Benvolio Montague and Tybalt Capulet, join in the fight. Then most of the inhabitants of the town join in and take sides, including the leaders of the two families and their wives.

✍ Cast the parts and read the scene aloud. Change the parts and read through the scene again.

Romeo and Juliet: from Act 1, Scene 1

GREGORY

 I will frown as I pass by, and let them take it as they
  list.

SAMPSON

 Nay, as they dare. I will bite my thumb at them.

ABRAHAM

 Do you bite your thumb at us, sir?

SAMPSON

 I do bite my thumb, sir.

ABRAHAM

 Do you bite your thumb at us, sir?

SAMPSON

 (*Aside to Gregory.*) Is the law of our side if I say 'Ay'?

GREGORY

 (*Aside to Sampson.*) No.

SAMPSON

 No, sir, I do not bite my thumb at you, sir. But I do
  bite my thumb, sir.

GREGORY

 Do you quarrel, sir?

ABRAHAM

 Quarrel, sir? No, sir.

SAMPSON

 But if you do, sir, I am for you. I serve as good a man
  as you.

ABRAHAM

No better.

SAMPSON

Well, sir.

(*Enter Benvolio Montague.*)

GREGORY

(*Aside to Sampson.*) Say 'better'. Here comes one of
   my master's kinsmen.

SAMPSON

Yes, better, sir.

ABRAHAM

You lie.

SAMPSON

Draw, if you be men. Gregory, remember thy
   swashing blow.

(*They fight.*)

BENVOLIO

Part, fools!
Put up your swords. You know not what you do.

(*Enter Tybalt Capulet.*)

TYBALT

What art thou drawn among these heartless hinds?
Turn thee, Benvolio, look upon thy death.

BENVOLIO

I do but keep the peace. Put up thy sword,
Or manage it to part these men with me.

TYBALT

What, drawn, and talk of peace? I hate the word
As I hate hell, all Montagues, and thee.
Have at thee, coward!

(*They fight. Enter three or four citizens with clubs or
   partisans.*)

CITIZENS

Clubs, bills, and partisans! Strike! Beat them down!
Down with the Capulets! Down with the Montagues!

(*Enter old Capulet in his gown, and his wife.*)

CAPULET

What noise is this? Give me my long sword, ho!

LADY CAPULET

A crutch, a crutch! Why call you for a sword?

(*Enter old Montague and his wife.*)

CAPULET

My sword, I say! Old Montague is come
And flourishes his blade in spite of me.

MONTAGUE

Thou villain Capulet! – Hold me not. Let me go.

LADY MONTAGUE

Thou shalt not stir one foot to seek a foe.

Clubs, bills, and partisans – weapons

The servants keep repeating the word 'sir'. In
what tone of voice do you think they say 'sir'?
How do you know that Sampson and Gregory
are keen to fight but are also nervous of doing
so? What is Benvolio's attitude to the fight?
What does he want the servants to do?

List the words or phrases which show that
Shakespeare wants us to know that Tybalt is full
of violence and enjoys fighting. How does Lady
Capulet mock her husband for thinking he is
still young enough to fight? What are both wives
trying to do?

Staging the fight

Unless you are trained in stage fighting, you will
have to find a very stylised and formal way of
staging the fight, rather than try to fight
realistically – which might result in someone
being hurt. Here are your ground rules:

1 Use your middle and forefingers as your
   sword.
2 Work in twos. Decide which of you is a
   Capulet and which a Montague. If your
   partner touches you with his/her forefinger,
   you must react because you have been hurt.
   Reactions are the most important part of
   stage-fighting: they make the fight seem more
   believable.
3 Plan a sequence of movements with your
   partner before you fight.

When you have planned your fight, two
pairs enter first and improvise the dialogue
between the servants. You may use the biting
thumb gesture or invent your own. Once the
fight is started, another pair enters as Benvolio
and Tybalt and improvises their dialogue. Then
the rest of the class enters as the citizens and
the Montagues and Capulets.

If you have two or three in the class who prefer
not to fight, they can read out the dialogue
while the rest mime the challenge and the fight.

What happens next?

You can see now how Shakespeare has built up the numbers on stage from three or four to as many as will fit on the stage, and from peace and quiet to noise and chaos. What should he do now? How long can the fight go on before the audience has had enough? How will Shakespeare stop the fight? Decide for yourselves before you read on.

⚡ Cast the parts and then read this extract.

⚡ In your groups, discuss the following:

1 What is the prince's attitude to the fighting and to his bloodthirsty citizens?
2 Shakespeare gives information through the prince about the background to the fight. What do we find out?
3 He also gives us a clue as to what happens in the play. What threat does the prince make and how might this threat be important to the plot?
4 How does the prince treat Capulet and Montague? What do you think he will say to them when he talks to them individually?

Act it out

⚡ Run through your fight scene again and, at a point you have already decided upon, have someone enter as the prince and either improvise his words or read the lines. Was the contrast between the noisy fighting and the citizens' silence as they listen to the prince effective as a piece of drama? What would you improve upon next time you tried the scene?

Benvolio's account

Lord Montague asks Benvolio for his account of how the fight started. Here is what Benvolio tells him.

BENVOLIO
    Here were the servants of your adversary
    And yours, close fighting ere I did approach.
    I drew to part them; in the instant came
    The fiery Tybalt, with his sword prepared;
    Which, as he breathed defiance to my ears,
    He swung about his head and cut the winds,
    Who, nothing hurt withal, hissed him in scorn.
    While we were interchanging thrusts and blows,
    Came more and more, and fought on part and part,
    Till the Prince came, who parted either part.

Does Benvolio's account fit with the impression you have of the fight? Is it an accurate account? Does it fit with the impression you already have of Tybalt?

(*Enter the Prince of Verona*)
The Prince angrily makes the crowd stop and listen to him.

PRINCE
    Rebellious subjects, enemies to peace,
    Profaners of this neighbour-stained steel –
    Will they not hear? What ho! you men, you beasts,
    That quench the fire of your pernicious rage
    With purple fountains issuing from your veins,
    On pain of torture, from those bloody hands
    Throw your mistempered weapons to the ground
    And hear the sentence of your moved prince.
    Three civil brawls, bred of an airy word
    By thee, old Capulet, and Montague,
    Have thrice disturbed the quiet of our streets,
    And made Verona's ancient citizens
    Cast by their grave-beseeming ornaments
    To wield old partisans in hands as old,
    Cankered with peace, to part your cankered hate.
    If ever you disturb our streets again,
    Your lives shall pay the forfeit of the peace.
    For this time all the rest depart away.
    You, Capulet, shall go along with me;
    And, Montague, come you this afternoon,
    To know our further pleasure in this case.

pernicious – wicked
moved – angry
cankered – rotten

Tybalt's account of the fight

Imagine you are Tybalt and have been asked by Lord Capulet to give your account of the fight. Write your account, making sure that you reveal your own character, Benvolio's character and your attitude to him. Where you can, use some of Shakespeare's words in your account.

A Tournament from *Pericles*

King Simonides has a fair daughter called Thaisa. On her birthday he summons princes and knights from all over the world to joust for her love. Whoever wins the tournament wins her hand in marriage. The scene begins with Simonides and Thaisa in seats of honour watching the knights in procession, each carrying a shield with his device or motto on it.

Pericles: from Act 2, Scene 2

(The first knight enters and passes by presenting his shield to Thaisa.)

SIMONIDES
Who is the first that doth prefer himself?

THAISA
A knight of Sparta, my most renowned father,
And the device he bears upon his shield
Is a black Ethiop reaching at the sun.
The word, Lux tua mihi.

SIMONIDES
He loves you well that holds his life of you.
(The second knight passes by.)
Who is the second that presents himself?

THAISA
A prince of Macedon, my royal father,
And the device he bears upon his shield
Is an armed knight that's conquered by a lady.
The motto thus in Spanish, Piu per dolcera che per forza.
(The third knight passes by.)

SIMONIDES
And with the third?

Lux tua mihi – you are my light
Piu per dolcera che per forza – more by gentleness than force

Your own mottoes

Now you carry on the scene, writing the script for the next three knights. Compose mottoes and symbols for the third, fourth and fifth knights.
Now continue the script with Thaisa's and Simonides' comments on the knights, trying to follow the pattern Shakespeare has set.

The sixth and last knight

How is the sixth knight different from the rest? (Look at the lords' sneering comments about him.)

(The sixth knight, Pericles, passes by.)
SIMONIDES
And what's the sixth and last, the which the knight himself
With such a graceful courtesy delivered?

THAISA
He seems to be a stranger, but his present is
A withered branch that's only green at top.
The motto, In hac spe vivo.

SIMONIDES
A pretty moral,
From the dejected state wherein he is,
He hopes by you his fortunes yet may flourish.

FIRST LORD
He had need better than his outward show.
Can any way speak in his just commend,
For by his rusty outside he appears
To have practised more the whipstock than the lance.

SECOND LORD
He well may be a stranger, for he comes
To an honoured triumph strangely furnished.

THIRD LORD
And on set purpose to let his armour rust
Until this day, to scour it in the dust.

In hac spe vivo – in this hope I live
show – appearance
whipstock – farmer's whip handle

Who do you think will win the tournament?
How do you know?

Staging the scene

The tournament is intended to celebrate Thaisa's birthday and so it needs to be performed as a ceremony, with each knight in turn coming up to the king and princess to show his loyalty and devotion. Props and music will help you achieve a sense of ceremony.

Making the shields   Work in six groups. Each group is responsible for making one of the six shields and creating the device. What you produce will depend upon your resources. You could use sheets of card or cardboard to make the shields. Silver or gold spray will give a royal finish. If you wish for a more glamorous effect, try papier mache.

Music   A ceremony is helped by music. If you do not have access to percussion instruments, use whatever is available – upturned waste-paper bins make good percussion. What can you do with chairs, desks, pencils, etc?
In groups, compose some rhythms to accompany the knights' procession. Will the sixth knight have a different rhythm? Combine the best ideas in each group for your final performance.

Acting out   First decide upon these points:

1 Who will play what part?
2 What will Thaisa and Simonides sit on? Wear?
3 How will you use the space that you have? Where will Simonides and Thaisa sit? Will Thaisa move? How will they greet the knights?
4 What will the knights walk from and to?
5 Where will the onlookers – the court – sit?
6 Who will perform the music? Where?

The speakers will need to know their lines well if they are not to stumble or have their eyes glued to the book.
When you are ready, try out the scene, making it as ceremonious as possible.

LOOK BACK

Did you succeed in creating the atmosphere of a tournament about to start? Did you make good use of the space you had to work in? What would you change or add if you were to do it again?

Write a newspaper report

Write a newspaper report describing the opening of the tournament. Make it a gossip column, with details about the knights and their mottoes and the mounting speculation and the bets taken about who will win.

What happens next?

The sixth knight – Pericles – wins the tournament. To Thaisa, he 'seems like diamond to glass'. But to the court he seems utterly unsuitable to marry their princess – until he tells them who he is. He says he is:

A gentleman of Tyre, my name is Pericles,
My education is in arts and arms,
Who looking for adventures in the world
Was by the rough seas reft of ships and men,
And after shipwreck driven upon the shore.

Why is his armour rusty? Is he suitable to marry a princess? Why is it not surprising that he is a gentleman?

Write the conversation between Thaisa and her father in which she begs him to let her marry the stranger knight.

4

STORMS AND TEMPESTS

—

Storms play a major part in Shakespeare's plays. Pericles was 'by the rough seas reft of ships and men'. Later in the play the rough seas reft him of his wife, Thaisa.

One of Shakespeare's plays is actually called *The Tempest* and it opens with a storm at sea. You will be studying this storm scene and another, from *Macbeth*, in this section of the book.

A storm at sea

The Tempest opens with a storm at sea. The master of the ship and his boatswain are doing their best to keep the ship afloat, while their passengers – Alonso, king of Naples, and his courtiers – make their job harder and try their patience.

⚡ In pairs or small groups, read the scene on page 32 aloud.

The Tempest: from Act 1, Scene 1

(*A tempestuous noise of thunder and lightning heard.*
Enter a Shipmaster and a boatswain.)

MASTER

Boatswain!

BOATSWAIN

Here, Master. What cheer?

MASTER

Good. Speak to the mariners. Fall to 't, <u>yarely</u>, or we
run ourselves aground. Bestir, bestir!

(*Enter Mariners.*)

BOATSWAIN

Heigh, my hearts! Cheerly, cheerly, my hearts! Yare,
yare! Take in the topsail! Tend to the master's
whistle! – Blow till thou burst thy wind, if room
enough.

(*Enter Alonso and his courtiers, Sebastian, Antonio,*
and Gonzalo.)

ALONSO

Good Boatswain, have care. Where's the Master? Play
the men.

BOATSWAIN

I pray now, keep below.

ANTONIO

Where is the Master, Boatswain?

BOATSWAIN

Do you not hear him? You mar our labour. Keep your
cabins! You do assist the storm.

GONZALO

Nay, good, be patient.

BOATSWAIN

When the sea is. Hence! What cares these <u>roarers</u> for
the name of king? To cabin! Silence! Trouble us not.

GONZALO

Good, yet remember whom thou hast aboard.

BOATSWAIN

None that I more love than myself. Down with the
topmast! Yare! Lower, lower! Bring her to try with
maincourse.

(*A cry within.*)

A plague upon this howling! They are louder than the
weather, or our office. Lay her ahold, ahold! Set her
two courses! Off to sea again! lay her off!

(*Enter Mariners, wet.*)

MARINERS

All lost! To prayers, to prayers! All lost!

BOATSWAIN

What, <u>must our mouths be cold</u>?

GONZALO

The King and Prince at prayers, let's assist them,
For our case is as theirs.

SEBASTIAN

I'm out of patience.

ANTONIO

We are merely cheated of our lives by drunkards.
This <u>wide-chapped</u> rascal – would thou mightst lie
drowning
The washing of ten tides!

(*A confused noise from within.*)

MARINERS

Mercy on us! – We split, we split! – Farewell my wife
and children! – Farewell, brother! – We split, we
split, we split! etc.

(*Exit Boatswain.*)

ANTONIO

Let's all sink with the King.

SEBASTIAN

Let's take leave of him.

(*Exit, with Antonio.*)

GONZALO

(Now would I give a thousand furlongs of sea for an
acre of barren ground. The wills above be done, but
I would <u>fain</u> die a dry death.

<u>yarely</u> – quickly
<u>roarers</u> – waves
<u>must our mouths be cold</u> – must we die
<u>wide-chapped</u> – big mouthed
<u>fain</u> – rather

32

How does Shakespeare make it clear that there is a lot of activity and confusion? Look particularly at the Boatswain's words. To set the atmosphere, Shakespeare has given the Boatswain words associated with ships – the jargon of sailors. Make a list of these words and phrases. What is the Boatswain's attitude to the king and his courtiers? How do you know he is impatient with them? Is the attitude of Sebastian and Antonio to their misfortune different from that of Gonzalo?

'What cares these roarers for the name of King?'

In this situation – a storm at sea – who has the most power or authority – the King, the Boatswain or the sea? What would you expect to be the normal order of authority or power?

Staging a storm

The scene is intended to be a noisy one, with sailors rushing about hauling on ropes and bringing the mast down.

In a group of ten or more, decide how you would stage the shipwreck to bring out the noise and confusion. Would the Boatswain be the most commanding person in the scene? Would he shout all his lines? What noises would you make to suggest a storm at sea? How would you suggest that the people on deck would find it difficult to stagger across the deck and would often be hurled to the floor by the violence of the wind.

'There's no harm done'

The ship sinks along with everyone on it – or so it seems. Two people on a nearby desert island have been watching the ship and its passengers – Prospero and his daughter, Miranda. Prospero was once Duke of Milan, a title now belonging to his brother Antonio, whom we met in the storm scene. In pairs, read the following extract from their conversation about the storm.

The Tempest: **from Act 1 Scene 2**

Enter Prospero and Miranda.

MIRANDA
If by your art, my dearest father, you have
Put the wild waters in this roar, allay them.
The sky it seems would pour down stinking pitch,
But that the sea, mounting to th'welkin's cheek,
Dashes the fire out. O, I have suffered
With those that I saw suffer! A brave vessel,
Who had, no doubt, some noble creature in her,
Dashed all to pieces. O, the cry did knock
Against my very heart! Poor souls, they perished.
Had I been any god of power, I would
Have sunk the sea within the earth, or ere
It should the good ship so have swallowed and
The fraughting souls within her.

PROSPERO
                                    Be collected.
No more amazement. Tell your piteous heart
There's no harm done.

MIRANDA
                              O, woe the day!

PROSPERO
                                    No harm.
I have done nothing but in care of thee,
Of thee, my dear one, thee my daughter, who
Art ignorant of what thou art, naught knowing
Of whence I am, nor that I am more better
Than Prospero, master of a full poor cell,
And thy no greater father.

MIRANDA
                                More to know
Did never meddle with my thoughts.

PROSPERO
                                          'Tis time
I should inform thee further. Lend thy hand,
And pluck my magic garment from me. – So,
Lie there, my art. – Wipe thou thine eyes. Have
   comfort.

th'welkin's cheek – the sky
fraughting souls – distressed passengers

33

⚡ In your groups, discuss the following:

1 What picture does Miranda give us of the storm? What is her reaction to the people she saw perish? What do you think Prospero means when he says 'There's no harm done'?

2 What evidence is there that Miranda does not know that her father was once an important person, a duke? And that therefore she has probably been on the island for most of her life?

3 What evidence is there that Prospero has supernatural powers and that he caused the storm?

Prospero's art

Prospero tells his daughter that he is rightful Duke of Milan. His brother Antonio tricked him and stole the title from him, and cast him and the baby Miranda out to sea in a 'rotten carcass of a butt' – an old tub. They drifted in the butt until they arrived on their isolated desert island.

Prospero then uses magic to put his daughter to sleep and calls up his familiar – the spirit Ariel who helps him perform his magic art.

⚡ In pairs, read aloud their conversation.

The Tempest: from Act 1, Scene 2

ARIEL

    All hail, great master! Grave sir, hail! I come
    To answer thy best pleasure, be't to fly,
    To swim, to dive into the fire, to ride
    On the curled clouds. To thy strong bidding task
    Ariel and all his quality.

PROSPERO

                      Hast thou, spirit,
    Performed <u>to point</u> the tempest that I bade thee?

ARIEL

    To every article.
    I boarded the King's ship. Now on the beak,
    Now in the waist, the deck, in every cabin
    I flamed amazement. Sometime I'd divide,
    And burn in many places. On the topmast,
    The yards, and boresprit would I flame distinctly,
    Then meet and join. Jove's lightnings, the precursors
    O'the dreadful thunderclaps, more momentary
    And sight-outrunning were not. The fire and cracks
    Of sulphurous roaring the most mighty Neptune
    Seem to besiege, and make his bold waves tremble,
    Yea, his dread trident shake.

PROSPERO

                      My brave spirit!
    Who was so firm, so constant, that this <u>coil</u>
    Would not infect his reason?

ARIEL

                        Not a soul
    But felt a fever of the mad, and played
    Some tricks of desperation. All but mariners
    Plunged in the foaming brine, and quit the vessel,
    Then all afire with me. The King's son Ferdinand,
    With hair up-staring – then like reeds, not hair –
    Was the first man that leaped; cried, 'Hell is empty,
    And all the devils are here!'

PROSPERO

    Why, that's my spirit!
    But was not this nigh shore?

ARIEL

    Close by, my master.

PROSPERO

    But are they, Ariel, safe?

ARIEL

                    Not a hair perished.
    On their sustaining garments not a blemish,
    But fresher than before; and as thou bad'st me,
    In troops I have dispersed them 'bout the isle.

<u>to point</u> – exactly
<u>coil</u> – confusion

What magic powers does Ariel have? How did he create the storm? What picture does he paint of the storm? How does his account differ from Miranda's account of the storm? How does he show pride in his ability to create thunder and lightning? How is it made clear that the relationship between Prospero and Ariel is that of master and servant?

What happens next?

You have learnt that Prospero has not really harmed the ship's passengers, as he promised his daughter, and that they are safe on the island.

In small groups, discuss why you think Prospero has chosen to have his brother shipwrecked on his island. What do you think will happen in the play? How might Prospero use his magic powers further?

Write a diary entry

Imagine you are Alonso, King of Naples, now shipwrecked on the island. Write your diary entry for the storm and the wreck. Look back at all three extracts from the play and use some of the language from them.

A storm as omen

Shakespeare often uses storms either to prophesy some terrible event to come or to show Nature's reaction to some terrible deed done by men. There is such a storm in *Macbeth*.

Macbeth has just secretly murdered Duncan, King of Scotland, while Duncan was staying at his castle. In the early morning, before the murder has been discovered, two lords, Lennox and Macduff, arrive to wake the king and prepare him for the next stage in his journey. While Macduff goes, as he thinks, to wake Duncan, Lennox engages the tense and guilty Macbeth in conversation about the unnatural storm that occurred in the night. Some time later, another lord, Ross, is talking to an old man about the night on which Duncan was murdered. In pairs, read the two conversations.

List the strange things that happened on that fatal night. How can you tell from Macbeth's only comment that he is feeling uneasy because he knows that Macduff will soon discover the murder? What evidence is there that Ross sees the strange events as the wrath of God and Nature? How do the old man's lines emphasise that such events are very unusual?

The language of horror

Part of the horror of these descriptions lies not just in the listing of the strange events, but in the language used to describe them.

In pairs, pick out the words and phrases which you think are most effective in conveying the horror.

In groups of four to six, take a line or a phrase each from one of the speeches and learn it. Then put the speech together by saying your phrases in turn. Try presenting the speech in different ways – whispering it, shouting it, saying it melodramatically, singing it, for instance. Which approaches did you find most effective?

Now as you say the lines, try acting out or dramatising in some way the strange events you are describing.

Macbeth: from Act 2, Scene 3

LENNOX
  The night has been unruly. Where we lay,
  Our chimneys were blown down, and, as they say,
  Lamentings heard i'the air, strange screams of death,
  – And prophesying, with accents terrible,
  Of dire combustion and confused events
  New-hatched to the woeful time. The obscure bird
  Clamoured the live-long night. Some say the earth
  Was feverous and did shake.
MACBETH
  'Twas a rough night.

Macbeth: from Act 2, Scene 4

OLD MAN
  Threescore and ten I can remember well;
  Within the volume of which time I have seen
  Hours dreadful and things strange; but this sore
      night
  Hath trifled former knowings.
ROSS
                            Ha, good father,
  Thou seest the heavens, as troubled with man's act,
  Threatens his bloody stage. By the clock 'tis day,
  And yet dark night strangles the travelling lamp;
  Is't night's predominance or the day's shame
  That darkness does the face of earth entomb
  When living light should kiss it?
OLD MAN
  'Tis unnatural,
  Even like the deed that's done. One Tuesday last,
  A falcon towering in her pride of place
  Was by a mousing owl hawked at and killed.
ROSS
  And Duncan's horses – a thing most strange and
      certain –
  Beauteous and swift, the minions of their race,
  Turned wild in nature, broke their stalls, flung out,
  Contending 'gainst obedience, as they would
  Make war with mankind.
OLD MAN
  'Tis said they ate each other.
ROSS
  They did so, to the amazement of mine eyes
  That looked upon't.

trifled – made trivial
knowings – occasions
stage – world
minions – darlings
contending – fighting

5

DEATHS

—

If you include all the battle scenes, hundreds, if not thousands, of people die in Shakespeare's plays. But each individual death is presented in a different way.

Foreseeing one's death

Richard of Gloucester wants to become king, but his elder brother, Clarence, stands in his way. He therefore imprisons Clarence in the Tower and makes plans to hire men to kill him there. The night before his murder, Clarence has a prophetic dream, that he has broken out of the tower and is escaping to France with his brother, Richard of Gloucester, when he falls overboard into the sea. (He does not realise that it is Richard who has imprisoned him.) The dream is prophetic because Clarence is about to be drowned in a butt (barrel) of Malmsey wine.

Richard III: Act 1, Scene 4

CLARENCE

Methought that I had broken from the Tower,
And was embark'd to cross to Burgundy;
And in my company my brother Gloucester,
Who from my cabin tempted me to walk
Upon the hatches: thence we look'd toward England,
And cited up a thousand heavy times,
During the wars of York and Lancaster,
That had befall'n us. As we pac'd along
Upon the giddy footing of the hatches,
Methought that Gloucester stumbled; and, in falling,
Struck me, that thought to stay him, overboard,
Into the tumbling billows of the main.
Lord, Lord! methought what pain it was to drown:
What dreadful noise of water in mine ears!
What sights of ugly death within mine eyes!
Methought I saw a thousand fearful wracks;
A thousand men that fishes gnaw'd upon;
Wedges of gold, great ingots, heaps of pearl,
Inestimable stones, unvalu'd jewels,
All scatter'd in the bottom of the sea.
Some lay in dead men's skulls; and in those holes
Where eyes did once inhabit, there were crept,
As 'twere in scorn of eyes, reflecting gems,
That woo'd the slimy bottom of the deep,
And mock'd the dead bones that lay scatter'd by.

main – sea
wracks – shipwrecks

In pairs, list the 'sights of ugly death' that Clarence sees at the bottom of the sea.

How does Shakespeare create a picture of something which is beautiful and repulsive at the same time?

Do you think he succeeds in making you feel the pain of drowning? Is it a particularly horrible way to die? Why?

The language

Make a list of the words Shakespeare uses to suggest that the cargoes of the wrecked ships are very precious and that they are now wasted and abandoned.

What is the effect on you of the image of jewels replacing the eyes in dead men's skulls? How do you think they are mocking the dead bones?

Use your imagination

If you can paint or draw, create a piece of art depicting Clarence's description of drowning at sea.

A picture of death

Write a piece in which you show how Shakespeare creates a vivid picture of death by drowning. Use quotations from the extract to illustrate your points.

A brave death

The house of Capulet is at war with the house of Montague. Tybalt Capulet has challenged Romeo Montague to a fight, but because Romeo is now married secretly to Tybalt's cousin, Juliet, he will not fight him. Mercutio, Romeo's friend, is appalled at Romeo's refusal to fight and accepts the challenge himself. Romeo tries to stop Tybalt and Mercutio fighting because the Prince has forbidden fighting on the streets on pain of death. Unfortunately, in trying to stop the fight, he allows Tybalt to thrust his sword into Mercutio under Romeo's arm. Mercutio dies, cursing the two houses and joking bitterly about the size of his wounds.

Romeo and Juliet: from Act 3, Scene 1

TYBALT
Romeo, the love I bear thee can afford
No better term than this: thou art a villain.

ROMEO
Tybalt, the reason that I have to love thee
Doth much excuse the appertaining rage
To such a greeting. Villain am I none.
Therefore farewell, I see thou knowest me not.

TYBALT
Boy, this shall not excuse the injuries
That thou hast done me. Therefore turn and draw.

ROMEO
I do protest I never injured thee;
But love thee better than thou canst devise
Till thou shalt know the reason of my love.
And so, good Capulet, which name I tender
As dearly as mine own, be satisfied.

MERCUTIO
O calm, dishonourable, vile submission!
'Alla stoccata' carries it away.

He draws his sword.

Tybalt, you ratcatcher, will you walk?

TYBALT
What wouldst thou have with me?

MERCUTIO
Good King of Cats, nothing but one of your nine lives.
That I mean to make bold withal, and, as you shall
use me hereafter, dry-beat the rest of the eight. Will
you pluck your sword out of his pilcher by the ears?
Make haste, lest mine be about your ears ere it be out.

TYBALT
I am for you.

He draws his sword.

ROMEO
Gentle Mercutio, put thy rapier up.

MERCUTIO
Come, sir, your 'passado'.

They fight.

ROMEO
Draw, Benvolio. Beat down their weapons.
Gentlemen, for shame! Forbear this outrage!
Tybalt, Mercutio, the Prince expressly hath
Forbid this bandying in Verona streets.
Hold, Tybalt! Good Mercutio!

*Tybalt under Romeo's arm thrusts his sword into
   Mercutio.*

A FOLLOWER
Away, Tybalt!

Exit Tybalt with his followers.

MERCUTIO
   I am hurt.
   A plague a'both your houses! I am sped.
   Is he gone and hath nothing?
BENVOLIO
   What, art thou hurt?
MERCUTIO
   Ay, ay, a scratch, a scratch. Marry, 'tis enough.
   Where is my page? Go, villain, fetch a surgeon.

                            Exit Page.

ROMEO
   Courage, man. The hurt cannot be much.
MERCUTIO
   No, 'tis not so deep as a well, nor so wide as a church
   door. But 'tis enough. 'T will serve. Ask for me
   tomorrow, and you shall find me a grave man. I am
   peppered, I warrant, for this world. A plague a'both
   your houses! Zounds, a dog, a rat, a mouse, a cat, to
   scratch a man to death! A braggart, a rogue, a villain,
   that fights by the book of arithmetic! Why the devil
   came you between us? I was hurt under your arm.
ROMEO
   I thought all for the best.
MERCUTIO
   Help me into some house, Benvolio,
   Or I shall faint. A plague a'both your houses!
   They have made worms' meat of me.
   I have it, and soundly too. Your houses!

             Exit Mercutio with Benvolio.

In pairs, take turns to explain to each other what Mercutio is saying from 'Ay, ay, a scratch . . .' to '. . . Your houses!' Explain also 'grave man', 'peppered', 'worm's meat'. What is the tone of 'but 'tis enough, 'twill serve'? What does the sentence which begins 'A braggart . . .' tell us about his attitude to Tybalt?

Mercutio curses the houses of the Capulets and the Montagues three times. In Shakespeare's time, it was believed that the curses of a dying man always came true. What do you think, therefore, might happen in the play?

Staging the scene

In fours, work out the moves needed for the fight. Then add the dialogue. The person playing Mercutio must put across his anger and bitterness at seeing his life ebb away.

You will find that it helps your understanding of Shakespeare and his language if you take the trouble to learn some of his lines. Learn Mercutio's dying speech – as much of it as you can.

A comic death

Shakespeare's audiences enjoyed watching someone die on stage. Actors and playwrights tried their hardest to move their audiences when they were writing or performing a death scene. In *A Midsummer Night's Dream*, Shakespeare makes us laugh by poking fun at the traditional melodramatic death scene. He has a group of simple country folk, who have never acted before, decide to present a tragedy that they have written themselves before the Duke to celebrate his wedding day. The plot of their play concerns Pyramus and his lover Thisbe who meet in secret because they are not allowed by their parents to marry. When Pyramus arrives at their meeting place, he finds Thisbe's mantle stained with blood and assumes she has been killed by a lion. So he kills himself. Thisbe then enters, finds her lover dead, and kills herself. Bottom the weaver plays Pyramus and Flute the bellows-mender plays Thisbe. (In Shakespeare's time women were not allowed to act.)

⚡ In pairs, act out the scene. Work out the movements you need from the words. Enjoy the exaggerated acting. Notice that Bottom is enjoying his death so much that he won't shut up and die, and that Flute is suffering so much from stage fright that he gets his words muddled.

A Midsummer Night's Dream: Act 5, Scene 1

BOTTOM *as Pyramus*

O wherefore, nature, didst thou lions frame,
  Since lion vile hath here deflowered my dear?
Which is – no, no, which was – the fairest dame
  That lived, that loved, that liked, that looked with
  cheer.
    Come tears, confound;
    Out sword, and wound
    The pap of Pyramus.
    Ay, that left pap,
    Where heart doth hop.
    Thus die I – thus, thus, thus.

He stabs himself.

    Now am I dead,
    Now am I fled;
    My soul is in the sky.
    Tongue, lose thy light;

              Exit Starveling at Moonshine.

    Moon, take thy flight;
    Now die, die, die, die, die.

                He dies.

FLUTE *as Thisbe*

    Asleep, my love?
    What, dead, my dove?
O Pyramus, arise.
    Speak, speak. Quite dumb?
    Dead, dead? A tomb
Must cover thy sweet eyes.
    These lily lips,
    This cherry nose,
These yellow cowslip cheeks
    Are gone, are gone.
    Lovers, make moan –
His eyes were green as leeks.
    O sisters three,
    Come, come to me
With hands as pale as milk;
    Lay them in gore,
    Since you have shore
With shears his thread of silk.
    Tongue, not a word!
    Come, trusty sword,
Come blade, my breast imbrue.

              She stabs herself.

    And farewell friends.
    Thus Thisbe ends.
    Adieu, adieu, adieu!

               She dies.

pap – breast
imbrue – pierce

6
PARENTS AND CHILDREN

—

You will find all of life in Shakespeare's plays, and all relationships – husbands and wives, lovers, brothers and sisters, kings and beggars. In this section, we shall choose one family relationship – that of parents and children – and look at how Shakespeare presents it.

Juliet and her father

Juliet has married Romeo secretly because her parents and his are enemies. Unfortunately their married happiness has been cut short because Romeo has been banished for killing Juliet's cousin in a duel. Unfortunately, too, Juliet's parents, Lord and Lady Capulet, have found a suitable husband for her – the Count Paris. They want to cheer her up for the death of her cousin and so have arranged the marriage to take place in three days' time, to Juliet's horror. Lord Capulet is angry at what he sees as her ingratitude in refusing to marry the Count.

In your groups, discuss the following:

What insults does Capulet hurl at his daughter? What does he threaten her with? Do you think he is over-reacting? What has made him so angry?

How does Juliet behave towards her father? Do you think she is frightened of him? Or that she is a very well brought-up girl? What does Lady Capulet think of her daughter's response to the marriage? What does she think of her husband's rage?

Romeo and Juliet: from Act 3, Scene 5

CAPULET
How now wife?
Have you delivered to her our decree?

LADY CAPULET
Ay, sir. But she will none, she gives you thanks.
I would the fool were married to her grave.

CAPULET
Soft! Take me with you wife.
How! Will she none? Doth she not give us thanks?
Is she not proud? doth she not count her blest,
Unworthy as she is, that we have wrought
So worthy a gentleman to be her bride?

JULIET
Not proud you have, but thankful that you have.
Proud can I never be of what I hate,
But thankful even for hate that is meant love.

CAPULET
How, how, how, how, chopped logic? What is this?
'Proud' and 'I thank you' and 'I thank you not'
And yet 'not proud'? Mistress minion you,
Thank me no thankings, nor proud me no prouds,
But fettle your fine joints 'gainst Thursday next
To go with Paris to Saint Peter's Church,
Or I will drag thee on a hurdle thither.
Out, you green-sickness carrion! Out, you baggage!
You tallow-face!

LADY CAPULET
Fie, fie! What, are you mad?

JULIET
Good father, I beseech you on my knees,
Hear me with patience but to speak a word.

CAPULET
Hang thee, young baggage! Disobedient wretch!
I tell thee what – get thee to church a'Thursday
Or never after look me in the face.
Speak not, reply not, do not answer me!
My fingers itch.

Fathers today

What does the scene tell us about the difference between a father's obligation towards his daughter in Shakespeare's time and his obligation today? What would make a modern father as angry as Capulet?

Does a father today expect as much obedience from his daughter as in Shakespeare's day?

The language

In pairs, read again the lines 'Soft, Take me . . .' to '. . . My fingers itch', ignoring Lady Capulet's interruption. Listen carefully to the different sounds and tone of voice used by the two characters. Try saying the lines in different ways until you know them off by heart. Which do you think is the best way of saying them?

What movements would you add? Would you have Juliet standing or kneeling? Would her father strike her? Would he face her or turn away?

Acting out the quarrel

In pairs, make a list of the insults Capulet hurls at his daughter. Take turns to play Capulet and shout the insults at your partner with as much anger and feeling as possible. The only thing your partner can say in reply is:

'Good father, I beseech you on my knees,
Hear me with patience but to speak a word.'

But you can say it as many times as you like.

In pairs, improvise and/or write a scene which provides a modern parallel about a father angry with his daughter. What are the equivalent modern insults? Threats?

Write Juliet's account in her diary of this scene with her father (use the language of the scene). Then write what you think she plans to do to escape the marriage. You may then want to compare your prediction by reading what Juliet actually does in Act 4, Scenes 1, 2, and 3 of *Romeo and Juliet*.

A similar scene: Egeus and Hermia

In *A Midsummer Night's Dream*, another father, Egeus, is angry that his daughter, Hermia, will not marry the man of his choice, who is called Demetrius, but wants to marry the man she loves, who is called Lysander. He asks the Duke of Athens to invoke the ancient law of Athens so that he may do as he wishes with his daughter.

A Midsummer Night's Dream: from Act 1, Scene 1

EGEUS
Full of vexation come I, with complaint
Against my child, my daughter Hermia.
Stand forth, Demetrius! My noble lord,
This man hath my consent to marry her.
Stand forth, Lysander! – And, my gracious Duke,
This man hath bewitched the bosom of my child.
Thou, thou, Lysander, thou hast given her rhymes,
And interchanged love-tokens with my child.
Thou hast by moonlight at her window sung,
Turned her obedience which is due to me
To stubborn harshness. And, my gracious Duke,
Be it so she will not here before your grace
Consent to marry with Demetrius,
I beg the ancient privilege of Athens:
As she is mine I may dispose of her;
Which shall be either to this gentleman
Or to her death, according to our law
Immediately provided in that case.
THESEUS
What say you, Hermia? Be advised, fair maid:
To you your father should be as a god;
Demetrius is a worthy gentleman.
HERMIA
So is Lysander.
THESEUS
In himself he is;
But in this kind wanting your father's voice,
The other must be held the worthier.
HERMIA
I would my father looked but with my eyes.
THESEUS
Rather your eyes must with his judgement look.

Set the scene up

⚡ In groups of five, each choose one of the roles in the scene. Decide where each one will be positioned. Where will Duke Theseus be to suggest his higher status? Will he sit or stand? Where will Egeus stand in relation to the two young men? Where Hermia? What tone of voice will each character use?
Now read through the scene. Is there anything you wish to change or add?

What happens next?

Do you think the Duke will decide in favour of Egeus or Hermia? What do you think will happen next in the play?

A comparison

Compare the scenes from *Romeo and Juliet* and *A Midsummer Night's Dream*. What similarities are there? What differences?

A piece of research

⚡ Are these fathers unfairly presented? Ask two or three fathers who you know have teenage daughters to read the two scenes. Then ask them to say whether they sympathised with or recognised the fathers' problem, or whether they thought that the fathers were being unreasonable. Is obedience in a daughter regarded as important now as it was in Shakespeare's time? How highly do today's fathers value obedience?

⚡ In your groups, discuss the following:

The two girls, Juliet and Hermia, find themselves in a similar situation: having to marry a man they do not love because their fathers expect it of them. Are there similar situations today? In what ways have women's lives changed since then?

Hamlet and his mother

Hamlet has come home from university to find his father, the king of Denmark, dead and his mother hastily remarried to his uncle. Alone, he talks of his disgust at his mother's remarriage.

Hamlet: from Act 1, Scene 2

HAMLET
    That it should come to this,
But two months dead, nay not so much, not two,
So excellent a king, that was to this
Hyperion to a satyr, so loving to my mother,
That he might not beteem the winds of heaven
Visit her face too roughly – heaven and earth
Must I remember? Why, she would hang on him
As if increase of appetite had grown
By what it fed on, and yet within a month,
Let me not think on't … frailty thy name is woman!
A little month or ere those shoes were old
With which she followed my poor father's body
Like Niobe all tears, why she, even she –
O God, a beast that wants discourse of reason
Would have mourned longer – married with my uncle,
My father's brother, but no more like my father
Than I to Hercules, within a month,
Ere yet the salt of most unrighteous tear
Had left the flushing in her galled eyes
She married. O most wicked speed … to post
With such dexterity to incestuous sheets!
It is not, nor it cannot come to good,
But break my heart, for I must hold my tongue.

⬆ Read the speech round your group, each person saying a line at a time. Now read it again with each person reading up to a punctuation mark. Which method of reading makes the meaning clearer to you?

⬆ In your groups discuss the following:

How long has Hamlet's father been dead? How long ago did his mother remarry?

Pick out three or four phrases which show Hamlet's disgust at his mother. Why do you think he exaggerates the speed of the marriage? What comparisons does he draw between his father and his step-father? Do you sympathise with his feelings about his mother's remarriage?

Improvise the scene

⬆ In groups of three, improvise the scene in which Hamlet returns home and meets his mother and his new father for the first time. Given what you know he feels, how do you think he will behave towards them? What will he say to them? What will they say to him?

⬆ Write up your scene in the form of a play. You may wish to compare your scene with Shakespeare's version in *Hamlet*: Act I, Scene 2, lines 64–120.

A family reunion

In *Pericles*, Prince Pericles and his wife Thaisa are travelling by sea when she goes into childbirth. At the same time, a great storm blows up. Thaisa dies having given birth to a baby girl. The sailors say that the storm will not die down until Thaisa's body is thrown overboard. Sadly Pericles agrees to this. He calls the baby Marina because she was born at sea and, because he is on his travels, leaves her with friends. After some years the news comes to him that she is dead. For years he mourns grievously, until he finds that the news was false and he is reunited with his daughter, now aged sixteen. They both go to the temple of the goddess Diana to give thanks for their reunion and discover that Thaisa's body was found on a shore and brought to life by a magician who is called Cerimon, who has kept Thaisa safe as a priestess in the temple. The play is not intended to be a realistic one but it captures the emotions of the reunited family very powerfully. Here is the scene in which the family are reunited.

Your own piece of drama

⬆ In groups of five or six, present the scene by having a narrator tell the story of the reunion in the temple while the rest of the group each take on the role of one of the characters and prepare a series of still pictures to accompany the narration. Bring out the fact that the family have been split up for sixteen years and that Marina thought she was an orphan.

Show your drama to the rest of your class and ask for their comments. Does presenting the scene in such a non-realistic way seem appropriate to the story?

Pericles: from Act 5, Scene 3

Enter on one side Thaisa and virgin priestesses of Diana, Cerimon, and other inhabitants of Ephesus; on the other side, Pericles, and Marina.

PERICLES

Hail, Dian! To perform thy just command
   I here confess myself the King of Tyre,
Who, frighted from my country, did wed
At Pentapolis the fair Thaisa.
At sea in childbed died she, but brought forth
A maid-child called Marina, who, O goddess,
Wears yet thy silver livery. She at Tarsus
Was nursed with Cleon, whom at fourteen years
He sought to murder. But her better stars
Brought her to Mytilene; 'gainst whose shore
Riding, her fortunes brought the maid aboard us,
Where, by her own most clear remembrance, she
Made known herself my daughter.

THAISA

Voice and favour!
You are, you are – O royal Pericles!

She faints.

PERICLES

What means the nun? She dies! Help, gentlemen!

CERIMON

Noble sir,
If you have told Diana's altar true,
This is your wife.

PERICLES

Reverend appearer, no;
I threw her overboard with these very arms.

CERIMON

Upon this cast, I warrant you.

PERICLES

'Tis most certain.

CERIMON

Look to the lady, O, she's but overjoyed.
Early one blustering morn this lady was
Thrown upon this shore. I opened the coffin,
Found there rich jewels, recovered her, and placed her
Here in Diana's temple.

THAISA

O, my lord,
Are you not Pericles? Like him you spake,
Like him you are. Did you not name a tempest,
A birth, and death?

PERICLES

The voice of dead Thaisa!

THAISA

That Thaisa am I,
Supposèd dead and drowned.

PERICLES

Immortal Dian!
O, come, be buried
A second time within these arms.

MARINA

My heart
Leaps to be gone into my mother's bosom.
She kneels.

PERICLES

Look who kneels here; flesh of thy flesh, Thaisa,
Thy burden at sea, and called Marina
For she was yielded there.

THAISA

Blest, and mine own.

PERICLES

Now do I long to hear how you were found,
How possibly preserved, and who to thank,
Besides the gods, for this great miracle.

THAISA

Lord Cerimon, my lord; this man
Through whom the gods have shown their power;
   that can
From first to last resolve you.

PERICLES

Reverend sir,
The gods can have no mortal officer
More like a god than you. Will you deliver
How this dead queen re-lives?

CERIMON

I will, my lord.
Beseech you first, go with me to my house,
Where shall be shown you all was found with her,
How she came placed here in the temple;
No needful thing omitted.

PERICLES

Lord Cerimon, we do our longing stay
To hear the rest untold. Sir, lead's the way.

Exeunt

wears yet thy silver livery – is still a virgin
yielded – born
deliver – explain

Remembering their courtship

🔸 Look at the scene from *Pericles* in Section 3 (pages 29–30), where Pericles wins the hand of Thaisa. Only nine months after that, they were separated. Write a conversation between Pericles and Thaisa in which they remember their courtship. Use words and ideas from the extract.

'Uneasy lies the head that wears a crown'

King Henry IV is dying. He is lying asleep on a bed with his crown set beside him on the pillow. His son, Prince Hal, sits with him. Hal has caused his father great sorrow: he spends his time drinking in taverns and keeping bad company, instead of in his father's council chambers, learning how to be a king. King Henry has just been mourning his son's behaviour to his other sons, saying that the blood weeps from his heart when he thinks of the rotten times to come when Hal is on the throne. His counsellor tries to comfort him by saying that Hal will cast off his low companions when he needs to – he is merely studying them at the moment so he will know how to rule them when he is king.

Now Hal and his father are alone in the room. Hal begins to think that his father's sleep is so deep that he must have died. He says farewell regretfully to his father, then lifts the crown and places it on his head.

Hal's thoughts

Two people take on the roles of Hal and King Henry while the rest of the group watches. Make a crown or find something which will suggest a crown. Mime the scene in which Hal sits by his father's bedside, thinks he has died, and slowly and carefully lifts up the heavy, gold crown of England and places it on his head. He sits thinking and then he leaves the room.

When the actors have played the scene once, the spectators can make suggestions to improve the scene. Other people might like to try the role of Hal.

After you have played the scene through a second time, decide what Hal might be thinking during the scene. Choose someone to speak these thoughts as the scene is played again.

The king awakes

How do you think the king reacts when he wakes up to find his crown and his son gone? Now read on.

Henry IV, Part II: from Act 4, Scene 5

(*The king calls for his other sons and his counsellors.*)

KING HENRY
    Where is the crown? Who took it from my
        pillow?

WARWICK
    When we withdrew, my liege, we left it here.

KING HENRY
    The Prince hath ta'en it hence. Go, seek him out.
    Is he so hasty that he doth suppose
    My sleep my death?
    Find him, my lord of Warwick; chide him hither.
    This helps to end me. See, sons, what things you are.

(*Warwick returns with this news:*)

WARWICK
    My lord, I found the prince in the next room,
    Washing with kindly tears his gentle cheeks.

KING HENRY
    But wherefore did he take away the crown?
    (*The Prince enters.*)
    Lo where he comes. Come hither to me, Harry.
    (*To counsellors*)
    Depart the chamber, leave us here alone.
    (*Pause as counsellors leave.*)

HAL
    I never thought to hear you speak again.

KING HENRY
    Thy wish was father, Harry, to that thought.
    I stay too long by thee, I weary thee.